Humanly Imperfect

ACCEPTING IMPERFECTIONS OF ONE'S SELF

BY DONTÁ FULLER

Contents

Preface

Writing about my perspective and experience on different topics has always been a thing for me. I wanted to try something different for this book. Writing about imperfection was not the easiest thing to do because you put yourself in an uncomfortable position to face reality and look at yourself in the mirror. Writing about a young black man showing imperfection and vulnerability is something I have not seen before. This is what inspired me to create this book. In perspective, I have always seen young black men struggle with being vulnerable, expressing their emotions and letting their guard down. I have struggle with this as well. Social environments have conditioned most of us to behave this way. This book represents a black man who is tired of holding back pain, imperfections, and unresolved feelings.

Imperfection is a scary thing to accept and I created this book to display that. 'Humanly' defines as a human feeling and from the point of view of a human. 'Imperfect' is the process of letting go any perfection and accepting the raw reality of who you are, your ups and downs of life, your true feelings and your mistakes that make you human. 'Humanly Imperfect' is accepting imperfection and speaking about life from the point of view of being human. It is the process of facing reality and accepting that you are an imperfect human.

This book consists of a collection of short stories, narrative poems, and short prose but it is telling a story about the character. Short prose is a narrative story that is shorter than short story. I have not written in short prose before, so this book shows it. I did not want to limit the character having one story line so the character shares more than one story written in short story, short prose, and narrative poetry form but all shares the same concept. The concept is centered around navigating through adulthood dealing with different experiences while channeling through vulnerability, personal development and accepting imperfections of one's self.

This book was written during the Covid-19 pandemic. The character tells his experiences as a process of accepting imperfections within himself. The character talks about his experience as a recent college graduate *(possibly hinting at dealing with a quarter-life crises)*, racial prejudice, heartbreak, practicing solitude, the covid-19 pandemic, family dysfunction, and personal development. As a recent college graduate, people struggle with finding their purpose in the world and experience a lot of trial and error at the start of their career. This character is no different. Even worse, being a black man who is finding their way is extremely challenging. The Covid-19 pandemic suddenly happened and affected everyone. From adjusting to a new normal, losing jobs and isolating yourself from loved ones became a challenge for many. Racial prejudice or bias is a constant issue, and a lot of black people feel scared or insecure about being black when it should not have to be that way. Dealing with heartbreak, relearning yourself, practicing solitude, working on personal development, and accepting your imperfections is a terrifying but rewarding process, especially for the character in this book. Overall, life is overly complex, but imperfection shows up very permanent for a human being.

Maya Angelou is one of few writers who has always been an inspiration of mines when it comes to writing. She was one of many writers who began the book genre 'Autofiction'. Autofiction is a term used in writing that describes someone recounting some of their life experiences in a story but adding parts of exaggeration and fiction. The term is more so like a fictionalized autobiography in a sense. Books like 'I Know Why the Caged Bird Sing' is one example of Angelou using autofiction. Autofiction is being used as one of the genres in this book. Some of the character's experiences mentioned in this story is like what I have experienced myself. I am channeling myself through some parts of the character's life experiences. I view this as the character sharing parts of his own life and sharing some parts that are similar to my life. The beauty of this story is revealing life for what it is and gaining perspective of how life challenges you to allow imperfection to show up in every way.

Introduction

I tell stories for fun, but this time I'm storytelling from the soul. I am a young black man who goes by the name of Je'Shaun. The nickname is Jez. Becoming an adult has not been easy for me. Being an adult has been tolerable if you must say. I have seen it all and I have yet to see more. I graduated from college and expected to become a successful, good paying salary black man. I found love and expected to live happily ever after. I thought the world would become a better, safer place for a black man like myself. I thought I would know my purpose in life when I glanced first at my college degree. I was wrong as wrong could get.

After graduating from UNC-Charlotte in Charlotte, North Carolina, I officially became an adult who is determined to become a successful graduate. That is until life hit me with some bullets and I found myself trying to do some intense recovery. Those same bullets forced me to humble myself and figure out my purpose in life. I am an insecure and vulnerable young black man. I am vulnerable to the pain I was exposed to in my professional and personal life. I am not secure being a young black man because I am scare to drive past a police car without thinking I am going to get pulled over. I am vulnerable because I am afraid to accept my mistakes, losses, and pain that makes me imperfect.

I am the definition of imperfect. I try so hard to act perfect in my life. In my eyes, Jez should be a strong black man that does not show vulnerability and is supposed to be at the top of his game in his life. I can fake it until I make it, but I can fake it until I can't take it. I just can't take this shit anymore. I'm tired of living a false reality of what my life is supposed to be, and I am ready tell my story of what my life is really like. I have sat alone with my own thoughts and feelings about what my life has been like. No more hiding it. No more perfection. I, Jez, am ready to accept my imperfections. Question is, Am I ready to accept that I am an imperfect black man?

I can't answer that yet until I tell my story and my perspective on things..

Quarter Life
Part I

Eyes are watery and crust flakes sit around my eyelids. The sunrise beams through the windows and my throat is dry from being dehydrated. I woke up feeling stress still thinking about the campus I just left. Graduating as a forty-niner with my bachelor's is exciting but leaving there with drama is not. I still cannot get over the experience I had as a Resident Advisor. My former boss making me do some of the staff's duties was unfair. She even lied and said if I refused to do the work, she would withhold my paycheck just so she can scare me. I hated that. A couple of my coworkers did not even have my back with all this happening, and I became almost everyone's lackey because my boss said so. I just wish my graduation time was not so dark.

Well, it is time for me to get ready for my internship. I love walking down Tyron street in Uptown Charlotte seeing successful people in their suits holding steamy hot coffee in their hands and getting off the light rail walking to some of the tall buildings. I kind of hope that will be me one day. Instead, I am going to start my third day at my copywriting internship. I sit at the computer doing my daily assignments as the assistant manager keeps hovering me over my shoulder asking me if I was doing okay. I sense something is off, but I pay it no attention. The assistant manager calls me to meet with him and the manager. We all sit down and talk about my experience here at the internship, even though it is only the third day. Before I know it, on my third day I was fired. I am confused, hurt, and more importantly, bruised. How could I get fired from my unpaid internship on the third day? How could they say my work is not good but didn't train me well enough to see if I could do great? The boss even says to me they hired too many interns, so I guess letting me go would be easy for them since I am not doing so well for them within three days.

Part II

I walk on my college campus, seeing all the students walk to their class. Some have smiling faces holding their freshly smelled Starbucks drink. Some have panic faces as they study last minute for a test. I start wishing that this can be me again so I can escape from this adult world. I walk upstairs looking at the symmetrical lines on the bricks. And I see my old boss from my RA job. I see the smile on her face, and I see the anger on mines reflecting from her eyes. Then, I wake up in pitch black dark realizing it was just a dream. As I wipe the drool from my mouth and flick an eye booger away, I wake up feeling like a failure and disappointed in myself. I did not leave college happy, and I am not starting post-undergrad life happy. I do not know where to find happiness. Should I keep trying to find happiness everywhere, or should I find it inside of myself?

Things start to turn around. I get hired as a teacher at this wonderful charter school. Expect everything to go so great. Then, one book fall from the shelf and my hopes turn into worries fast. The principal is the principal from hell. I cannot do my job like how Jez should do his job without being micromanaged. It seems like my reoccurring fear of being at another job is starting to resurface again. I decide to stand up for myself about the principal's micromanaging ways. And guess what? On the last day of school, I get fired for voicing some of my concerns. It feels like I hit rock bottom again. Seeing my letter of termination being slapped on the table by the principal is so disheartening. I run to my classroom, cry my eyes out and left the building. I did not want to look back just like how I did not want to look back at my RA job or internship.

I stayed in my house for days. I did not bathe, and I was ashamed to tell anyone I was fired. The must from the armpits distracted me from losing my job. I am supposed to be this hard-working man who just got his bachelor's degree. I am supposed to be a young, successful black man who is supposed to have their shit together. Who am I kidding? I guess this is not the average dream of a recent graduate. My fear of being unsuccessful and being less valuable is validated AGAIN. After allowing Indeed.com to become my best friend, I land another teaching job at another school. Everything seems so perfect like before. But after a few months, things change in the blink of an eye. The school gets shut down due to financial hardships. Losing two jobs within a year span, I was past the scale of 1-10 of feeling embarrassed and ashamed. I wanted to fill in that void of believing I should be a successful young black man who has a college degree. Instead, I was lying in bed feeling sad and ashamed.

A degree could not prepare me for this kind of challenge. Goals I created could not keep me motivated to figure out my next steps. The color of my skin validated my failures and fears to become successful. A strong voice I use to express myself and a posture that I have like nobody else is still taking advantage of. What am I useful for? What is this voice and posture useful for? What am I useful for in this world?

Part III

The two feet that are planted on this ground must walk in one direction or the other. One path is still trying to figure out what I want for myself, and the other path is going towards a dead end. I decide to take the path of figuring things out. Losing another job at another school took a blow to my head. I can't believe it was happening to me again. I feel embarrassed, but I am not going to for long. I decide to take a walk at the park to think about things. I look at the sky and see the clouds move. The clouds end up blocking the sun from shining. I stare for a minute and wonder why the clouds are doing that. Then, I look at myself and question my purpose on this earth.

As I question my purpose on this earth, I question if I will ever succeed as a black man. I question if I should try again to risk myself being at rock bottom. I question if I will find the right job that will keep me stable. And I question if I will recover from these failures. I continue to look in the sky and figure out what future path is best for me. I take a deep breath and close my eyes. I let go of this idea of trying to be a young successful black man. I start to accept that I am a young black man who is building himself to become successful. Losses and failures are part of being successful. Leaving college made me realize this is only the beginning. I had a bad experience being an RA. I lost an internship and two jobs. I became an obsessed human who wanted this perfect life.

I allowed my fears of being viewed as less valuable and less successful to disappoint me the most. I allowed myself to become a young black man who fears being viewed as a threat in the workplace. I allowed myself to become a young black man who fears being outspoken so I can grow professionally and be treated kindly. And I allowed myself to become a young black man who fears failing again. I, Jez, will start being kind to myself. I will let my fears go and keep trying. Wherever I go, I will not give up with confidence and not fear trying to become successful.

I Won't Surrender

As a black man, I feel scared, insecure, and not safe. As an innocent child born into this country, I am perceived as a threat. As an innocent child born into this country, I believe we are all supposed to love one another and see no color. As a black man living in this country, I am perceived as being unsuccessful. As a black man living in this country, I am supposed to follow the rules and surrender my skin color to please folks. As a black man living in this country, I am insecure because my success is at risk of failing, and my safety is threatened because prejudice is spreading like a wildfire. As a black man, I should not have to surrender to anything, and I should move regularly like any other human...

I am a threat by default,

My skin is dangerous on the outside,

But the beautiful color resembles in people's eyes.

I am outspoken and honest,

But my words to certain people do not come off as ironic.

My skin feels so warm and soft,

Its brownness and color blends in with the sunlight than
the dark.

Why am I perceived as a threat?

Why do police officers want to put a gun to my neck?

Why is my skin so dangerous?

I have all these questions,

But no one can answer it.

I won't surrender!

I won't surrender!

I want to be an American who is black,

And in the picture.

Humanly Imperfect

My color,

My voice,

My personality,

Is a non-choice.

Why do you hate us?

But we are force to love you.

How do you perceive us?

When the world does not care how they perceive you.

I'm tired of being mad,

I'm tired of being scared,

I'm tired of shielding my blackness,

And I'm tired of surrendering to your fear.

I won't surrender!

I won't surrender!

I want to be an American who is black,

And in the picture.

Ms. Rona

I am a mad citizen whose world has changed in the blink of an eye. Nobody, and I mean nobody was doing anything wrong and suddenly, a bitch who is called the coronavirus, or COVID-19, just appears in the United States without warning. This bitch made me stay at home, work from home, workout from home, deal with my problems at home, and use zoom from home and keep me away from my family and friends. I decided to talk about how this invisible hoe changes my life and this world for the worse...

Humanly Imperfect

Dear Ms. Rona,

You creeped into the United States with no hesitation,

You made a lot of people sick-

And made citizens lack ventilation.

You affected my job in many ways,

From working on zoom and telehealth,

And decreasing my biweekly pay.

You caused people to go crazy,

Taking all the water and toilet paper,

And making others lose their sanity.

Ms. Rona,

You blinded our leader's intelligence,

Causing the country to lack any excellence.

Everything shuts down,

And we are order to stay at home,

I am dealing with a broken soul,

While everything outside is put on hold.

Humanly Imperfect

I want the madness to stop,

I want to go back to 2019,

When everything was normal or what not.

Now everything is changing,

I see more of my laptop,

Than I see parking lots.

Ms. Rona, I have some good news to tell you!

Face mask became my best friend overnight.

I can't believe I have to wear this shit,

I can barely learn how to breathe,

Even my stinking ass breath does not agree.

I asked the clerk the other day how much is their juice,

And she says she cannot understand me.

Ms. Rona,

This world has gone crazy,

The media creating this hysteria is scary.

Humanly Imperfect

Prejudice behavior is still happening to people that are my
skin color,

Health disparities are getting worse as you jump from
person to person,

And the death rates have worsened.

Ms. Rona, Ms. Rona

Go away!

And do not come back again another day.

I want my life to be normal,

I want to be more social.

I want the hysteria to stop,

I want to be able to shop.

I want to stop sulking in all this pain in my apartment,

I want to stop doing workouts on this dusty ass carpet.

Unemployment keeps rising,

Suicide deaths are becoming more likely,

We need you to leave so our world can again start shining.

Humanly Imperfect

I want to hug my mom again,

I want to see my nephew walking.

Ms. Rona,

Please leave us alone!

Yours truly,

A mad citizen!

Heartbreak Rehab

I experienced heartbreak. I experienced a breakup that hurt in the worst way. I express myself in the honest way possible. I am showing vulnerability in the honest way possible. I am showing feelings that make me uncomfortable. I am releasing this pain so that it will make me feel okay. I am expressing my story to get through this pain. While dealing with this pain, I enter a stage of learning how to be alone and taking a good look at myself as a human being. While it is needed, it has been difficult, to say the least...

Part I… My Love Goes Deep Within

My love goes deep within,

Even after the heartbreak,

It is so hard to pretend.

I can still feel your body against mines,

I can still remember how your kiss taste,

And how your love felt like beautiful fine wine.

I can remember the kind words you used to describe me,

I remember the anger you felt at times as passion for me,

But I also remember you told me you wanted to do you and be free.

Our love was created so strong and so powerful,

I do not understand why you would damage it so foul.

Our bond goes deep beyond a friendship,

A relationship,

A partnership,

Yet, you turned it off like a light switch you just flick.

My love goes deep within,

My love for you will always be the same,

But I cannot promise it will not change.

Part II

Feelings are moving like a hurricane circling around one
state,

One minute I am fine,

The next, I am in an empty space.

Why can't I burn this pain away?

I want to feel fine and be able to say I am okay.

Why heartbreak cannot feel any easier?

Why emotions trick the mind so faster?

I want to be alone, but I want a body close to me,

I want to fill a void that you left because you wanted to be
free.

It feels unhealthy to try to keep close to you,

Choosing myself means you must lose me too.

Feelings are moving like a hurricane circling around one
state,

One minute I am heartbroken,

The next, my mind emotionally shakes.

Look in the mirror and my eyes are red,

My tears wet the top of my shirt,

And my heart is hurting my head.

I see the pain in my face, posture, and lips,

I cry so hard,

I want to punch the mirror until it slips.

I walk around my apartment and look at pictures of us,

I smile on the inside,

But on the outside,

The reality hits me so tough.

You broke up with me so randomly,

While a guy was flirting with you,

And giving you attention to ease your own sanity.

We walked together in a park while you were breaking my
heart,

Humanly Imperfect

You kept rejecting me afterwards like a repeating sound of
a fart.

Social media and thinking of other guys were not our
downfall,

Your problems and feelings of self,

created our last haul.

Look in the mirror again and my eyes are red,

My tears wet the top of my shirt,

And my heart is hurting my head.

I see my pain when I look at pictures of you,

And realize us being apart is true.

Part III

Darkness crowds my eyes,

As I sit here and cry,

I go to sleep wondering if you are lying next to some new
dude,

As I do not think this would come true.

I have nightmares of this happening,

Causing me not to sleep,

Then I drink a glass of sweet wine just relaxing.

I'm trying so hard to get over you,

I can't help but to think if you are possibly with someone
new.

I feel abandoned,

I feel hurt,

How could you do this to me?

I wouldn't have done this to you.

My love for you cuts deep like a knife,

After all, I always stood by your side.

Never was I perfect,

But fighting for our love was worth it.

I attempted to do everything I could to be close with you,

Even after we broke up,

And you were disrespectful and rude.

I didn't want to lose what we had,

I just wanted to stop feeling sad.

I have to accept that you are moving on,

I have to tell myself to be strong,

I wrote letters but sending them to you would be wrong.

I wonder if our love was ever real to you,

I wonder if it was real when you called me your boo.

I replaced rose pedals with tears overnight,

I cried I cried because it felt good and right,

But as the darkness crowd my eyes,

I stopped putting up a fight.

Part IV

It won't hurt to shed one more tear,

It won't hurt to temporarily disappear,

It won't hurt to see a picture of us again without fear.

I laid in bed and cried,

I kept wishing that my heart could heal overnight,

I still felt you close to me by my side,

I still hoped I could increase your sex drive.

Every day I get up and think it's a nightmare,

I prayed that we could still be together,

I lied to myself thinking it was over,

In my heart, I still feel like your lover.

Imperfectly saw through,

Looked out and saw the real you,

Humanly Imperfect

Accepting this reality is true,

Soon, soon, soon,

I will heal and my heart will be good as new.

Each day feels like a brick is hitting my face,

I miss the feeling of you rubbing my chest,

And giving me a taste.

I tried so many things to not feel this pain,

I hooked up with a couple of people,

But one sexual moment I ended up almost calling your

name.

I did everything I could to get you out of mind,

But my heart would remind me of you every time.

Dealing with this pain isn't easy,

Dealing with this pain isn't perfect,

I find myself watching you all the time,

And then the pain I feel starts hurting.

Humanly Imperfect

I stared at a photo of us as I cried,

My emotions got the best of me too many times.

I wanted to text you,

I wanted to scream at you,

I wanted to tell you how much I love you,

I wanted to get over you by finding somebody to date and
screw too.

I have a feeling you won't change your mind,

So I try to get over you,

I have a feeling you may change your mind,

So I don't let go of my hope too soon.

I watch the rain thump my window,

Thinking about where we are right now,

I watch darkness in my room,

Trying to clear my thoughts of you,

Without hearing a sound.

I vented to friends so many times,

It made me feel better,

But I still wanted you by my side.

I sat in a car by myself,

Thinking something is wrong and I need some help.

I have accepted that I am a man deeply in love going
through pain,

But I know for myself this will eventually make a personal
change.

Each day feels like the sun gets brighter hitting my face,

I miss the feeling of being happy,

I found the love I can give to myself for a change.

I try so many times to accept reality,

Each day gets better,

But there is no definite finale.

I will do everything to keep you in my heart,

But I have to keep healing to have a fresh start.

Hello Loneliness

I sit in my bedroom hearing the car honking sounds
coming from outside,

I am recovering from heartbreak, but I don't know where
my feelings lie,

I force myself to be by myself,

Eat by myself,

Sleep by myself,

But being by myself does not feel great sometimes.

I reflect on my decisions and sit with dissatisfaction,

I am forced to grow as I increase my awareness,

I look on social media and see people show greatness,

But I sit here accepting that I am not perfect.

Even though I am by myself,

I know I am not by myself,

But at times I still feel like I am by myself.

I see people who are scared to be alone,

Meaning not have someone close to them 24/7 to feel
whole,

Why I wanted to cry when my lover did not validate me at
times?

Or when some family members did not notice me,

Causing me to want to hide.

Heartbreak causes others to be bitter and by themselves,

I am not going down that road,

I want to be happy and have good health.

I see a stranger named Cala who is weeping on a comfy
bench,

She has tears on her blouse, and it is decorated by lent.

She is scared and feeling lonely because her boyfriend
broke up with her and went to the army,

Her mom and dad don't live in the same city as her,

And her friends are always busy.

A new guy she hooked up with rejected her because she
quickly wanted a title,

The new guy thought she was nuts and wild.

She tells her Facebook friends she is lonely and single,

Guys slide her DM's on Instagram, but it is not enough for
her.

I see a guy named Derek reading a comic book at a table
outside of Five Guys,

He writes that he loves his alone time,

And he knows the reason why.

He spends time reflecting,

And spends time growing,

He loves his own company,

And does not need anyone to fill in voids of his emotions
and sanity.

He is recovering from cutting family ties,

And he is staying single until he finds the right one who
will want to invest their time.

I see people vent to social media,

Humanly Imperfect

I see people use distractions to hide their growing phobias.

I walk around and see people live normal lives,

But I always wonder what people really feel deep down
inside.

As I lay on bed thinking about what is ahead,

I can't help but to feel alone mentally in my head,

I'm actually alone but not alone physically,

I have people who still love me.

Reading what's on social media really has me thinking,

What could all these people really be feeling,

Some want relationships,

And some attention,

And some just want others to just listen.

Loneliness reveals your imperfections,

But constant attention will reveal your need to show
perfection.

A coffee date at Starbucks by yourself will not hurt right?

A table for one dinner at Olive Garden will not bite.

Humanly Imperfect

Being alone equates reflection,

And reflection reveals imperfections.

What I see is nothing wrong with being lonely,

We all need to time to practice,

Nobody is not going to heal me,

I can only heal me,

But people around us need to be listening.

Being lonely is having no one at all,

Being alone is supporting yourself but having support
when you fall.

I smile and frown every day,

Knowing that I am not perfect in any way,

I sit by myself,

Telling myself I am going to be okay,

Someone needs to know that being alone sometimes can
help you become great.

The Fam

My dream of being in a perfect family is far from reality. Dysfunction has crept into my family life in many ways. I express my desire of wanting to be loved correctly by some of my family. I desire to want no fake love from some of my family. I desire to not feel sad anymore because of some of my family. I desire to break incorrect generational ways of love from some of my family. I desire to not normalize toxicity with some of my family. I just desire real love from some of my family...

Humanly Imperfect

Love is not supposed to be like this,

Love is not supposed to have distance in it.

Love is not supposed to create animosity,

Love is not supposed to have toxicity.

Family is here for me when it is not convenient,

Family supports me even when I cannot pay my own rent.

Family is not supposed to leech off me every chance they
get,

Family stays together and get over problems with quick
fix.

I relive moments of when I did not feel the love,

I still feel those moment in my 20's like a kid who used to
scrap their knees on the rug.

Not showing up for those big days,

Posting comments on Facebook acting like everything is
okay.

I relive moments of when I sat in my cap and gown and
pout,

I still feel those moments in my 20's like an angry kid
who saw their parent jump to another spouse.

I am tired of being viewed the bad guy,

While you, family, play the victim and lie.

I am still a man who needs consistent love,

As family when you don't do that,

It boils my blood.

I had to go to counseling to heal from this type of love,

I wish I always didn't feel like I need a hug.

I took a swim to drown in this heartbreaking pain,

I need to know what it feels like to lose a battle once
again.

Every day I felt guilty for leaving family behind,

But who was feeling sorry for me when I was embarrassed
on a big day for the second time?

Humanly Imperfect

Family is only a word,

The meaning behind it creates an impactful verb.

I'm tired of hearing "life is too short",

Was life too short when you decided to stab me in the
back with a fork?

Call me dramatic, but I'm hurt,

I forgive you but I'm still hurt,

I kicked dirt in a kid's face because he receives support
from family,

I envy his blessings,

And he looks at me like I am crazy and need counseling.

I depended on friends to give me family love,

I depended on House of Payne to give me family laughs,

I depended on childhood pictures to show me those
moments again,

I depended on venting talks to help me see the positive of
family again.

Love is cherished,

Love is beautiful,

When it comes from family.

I am in my twenties,

Still needing to be love correctly from family.

Changes come and changes go,

But family is supposed there when you need them the
most.

I... Let Go

Staring at the grass that is covered in frost,

I let go of the fact that the grass is going to be wet.

An accidental cut on my skin from shaving my facial hair,

I let go accepting that I am going to have a scar for a while.

Burned the chicken that was cooking on the stove,

I cooked before but doing chicken was my first try,

I let go of being hard on myself and realize I can do better next time.

Forgot my Chapstick at home while rushing to leave for work,

I let go of wanting to go back home to get it and left my lips ashy and chapped for the day.

Missed my exit on the highway because I was thinking about what I am going to eat for lunch today,

I let go of being mad at myself and just rerouted.

Cried on an incredibly special day of mines,

When I tried to make everything so perfect and fine,

I let go of trying to be happy and let myself be sad.

Tried to take my own life when everything seems so dark,

I let go of that decision and fight my way to see the light.

Mind plagued with suicidal thoughts,

Thought I was crazy,

Thought I needed medicine,

Or a psychiatric unit to lay in,

I let go of calling myself insane and seek therapy to be
okay.

Hearing people say all the time "you will get over it" or
"you need to let it go",

I let go of what people say and let myself heal at my own
pace.

Had to leave some people I love behind,

Too much toxic energy was weighing down on my life,

I let go and realized love does not equal being treated
shitty.

Chased after some people who did not chase after me,

Kept trying to fight in some relationships when those
people were not fighting with me,

I let go and nurtured my self-worth.

Professional life has been a mess,

I just want to get away sometimes and rest,

I let go of workaholic tendencies,

and became more obsessed in self-care routines.

Life is running in constant circles,

I fight everyday to be the best I can be,

Reality is something I always neglect,

I… let go of trying to be perfect.

Humanly Imperfect

A beautiful black man with scars in my soul.

Beautiful on the outside,

But imperfect on the inside.

Mistakes were made on days I was not sane,

Mistakes were made by people who caused me pain.

My pain does not define me,

But my own strength scares me.

My imperfections are permanent every day,

I am imperfect in every way.

I give myself time to heal from things,

I even act out sometimes when the pain stings,

Heart has been broken many times,

Humanly Imperfect

My imperfections allow the bandage sealed on my heart to
unseal and fly.

As I close my eyes and imagine a blank space,

I see myself standing in a mirror looking at my own face.

As I open my eyes and see an imperfect man,

I stare with a smile for as a long as I can.

A beautiful black man whose soul is imperfect.

I am a human who-

Loves imperfectly,

Heals imperfectly,

Shows vulnerability imperfectly,

And accepts pain imperfectly.

I am humanly imperfect.

Conclusion: Accepting My Imperfections

I am a 24-year-old man who is imperfect. I am imperfect in every way. I have my fears of what is to come in this world, but I want to say my fears out loud. I don't want to fail but I don't want to keep being scared of the unthinkable. My vulnerability defines my strength. My pain excels into greatness. My struggles coming out of college tells me what success looks like. Success is knowing what you bring to the table and not allowing anybody to steal the confidence you have for what you bring. Seeing the world become unpredictable and challenges show how imperfect this world is. The world can endlessly show imperfection so why can't I? I feared being imperfect. I was scared of accepting my imperfections. I was scared to face reality. I was scared to face myself in the mirror as an imperfect person.

I've spoken with a guy named Freddie. He was black just like me. He is 24 years old just like me. And he was moving through life just like me. He told me his story on how he had to accept that he is imperfect and how he had to go through challenges in his life to accept everything around him is imperfect. He was afraid of being imperfect just like me. He became unhappy with everything in his life. He left his job because his boss told him the job could not add a traveling incentive for him to do business on the road from time to time. He moved out of his father's house and got his own apartment because he felt uncomfortable still living with his dad. He picked up another job where a traveling incentive was included. He broke up with his ex-girlfriend of two years because things were not exciting to him like they used to be, and he decided to date someone else a few weeks after who brought the excitement in his life again. He worked hard for everything to be perfect in his life and he would accept no type of shortcomings.

Things started to turn horrible for Freddie. His new job shut down after working there for a few months due to the company having financial hardships. His new girlfriend broke up with him after he lost his job and he found out she was using his bank card a few times without him knowing and without permission to go shopping. He did not have a secure savings plan for a place to live. Due to him not being able to pay his rent, he moved out of his apartment and moved back in with his father. He ended up in a spot bad and could not believe this was happening to him. His insecurities led to him losing everything imperfect to him. He lost his job, his ex-girlfriend, his apartment, and his imperfect self. He realized that his expectations were not reality. The reason he did not accept the imperfections around him because he did not find gratitude in what he had and didn't want to deal with reality. He told me that in order to keep accepting the imperfections you have, you have to continue releasing ideas of being perfect and keep accepting the realities of imperfection everywhere around you, including yourself. His words really stuck with me.

I release the idea of being perfect. I release my unrealistic expectations into the air. I release the pain that I feel inside. I release my vulnerability and let it show on the surface. I release the fear of being a black man not feeling safe or going to succeed. I allow my fears and insecurities to show on the surface. I, Jez, am ready to stop being obsessed with the idea of faking shit. I, Jez, am ready to be strong again.

I am imperfect. I was born imperfect. I live in an imperfect world that I am imperfect in. I will forever be imperfect. I am in an imperfect I am human. I am a human who fights to show perfection. I am a human who makes mistakes. I am a human who goes through pain. I am a human who allowed people to cause me pain. I am a human who pushed some away. I am a human whose trauma is still unresolved. I am a human whose mental health is scar. The reality of all of this is my life is imperfect. The reality of my experiences proved that I am not perfect. The reality of myself shows that I need to accept my life for what it was and what it is now. I am ready to accept that I am a black man who is... humanly imperfect!

Author's Notes

The subject in this book is about revealing your imperfections and accepting them. The short stories, short prose and narrative poems in the book all tell different stories about the character Jez but show the same message. I wrote this book in creating a message to myself and everyone else that life is all about allowing yourself to be human. By allowing yourself to be human, you have to mess up, go through pain, deal with life challenges, and build yourself to become better.

Sometimes it is easy to forget to be kind to yourself when something happens to you. It is easy to crave perfection when you vision your life in false reality. It is easy to deny imperfection because we are too embarrassed, ashamed, and uncomfortable about it.

Different topics in this book show how real imperfection is. It shows how imperfect I am. It shows how imperfect Jez is. And it shows how imperfect everyone else in this world is. Imperfection is beautiful. Learn how to be kind to yourself for your imperfections.

Index

www.ingramcontent.com/pod-product-compliance
Lightning Source LLC
Chambersburg PA
CBHW070606160726
48003CB00005B/2133